# COUNTRIES

# Egypt

Alice Harman

# Explore the world with **Popcorn -** your complete first non-fiction library.

Look out for more titles in the Popcorn range. All books have the same format of simple text and striking images. Text is carefully matched to the pictures to help readers to identify and understand key vocabulary.
www.waylandbooks.co.uk/popcorn

Published in paperback in 2014 by Wayland
Copyright © Wayland 2014

Wayland
Hachette Children's Books
338 Euston Road
London NW1 3BH

Wayland Australia
Level 17/207 Kent Street
Sydney NSW 2000

Produced for Wayland by
White-Thomson Publishing Ltd
www.wtpub.co.uk
+44 (0)843 208 7460

Editor: Alice Harman
Designer: Clare Nicholas
Picture researcher: Alice Harman
Series consultant: Kate Ruttle
Design concept: Paul Cherrill

British Library Cataloging in Publication Data
Harman, Alice.
   Egypt. -- (Popcorn countries)
   1. Egypt--Social conditions--Juvenile literature.
   2. Egypt--Social life and customs--Juvenile literature.
   3. Egypt--Geography--Juvenile literature.
   I. Title II. Series
   962'.056-dc23

ISBN: 978 0 7502 8333 5

Wayland is a division of Hachette Children's Books,
an Hachette UK company.
www.hachette.co.uk

Printed in Malaysia

10 9 8 7 6 5 4 3 2 1

Picture/Illustration credits: Alamy: Philip Game 20; World Religions Photo Library 21; Peter Bull 23; Stefan Chabluk 4; Corbis: front cover Tuul/Robert Harding World Imagery; DiMaggio/Kalish 13; Franz-Marc Frei 14; Dreamstime: Happykimmyj 17b; Getty: AFP 9; Frans Lemmens 18; Robert Harding: age footstock 10; James Strachan 12; Shutterstock: Bzzuspajk 5; Dan Breckwoldt 6; javarman 7; bumihills 8; Zdenek Krchak 15; Louise Cukrov 16; O.Bellini 17m; bonchan 17t; Rich Carey 19; Carsten Reisinger 22; WTPix 11.

# Contents

# Where is Egypt?

Here is a map of Egypt.
Most of Egypt is in north-east
Africa. Part of Egypt is in Asia.

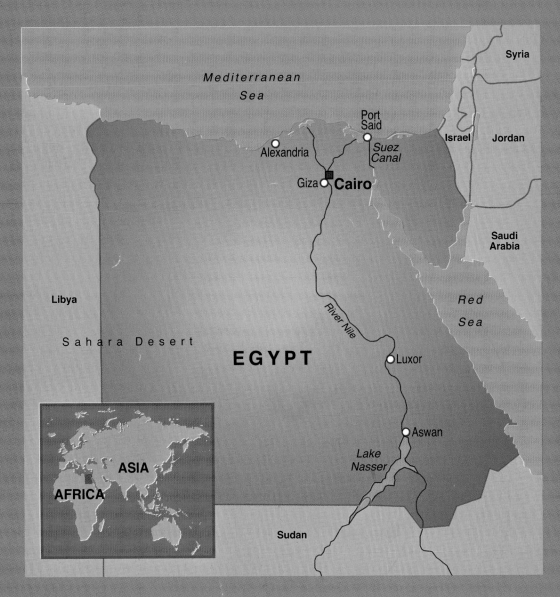

Cairo is the capital of Egypt.
It is in the north of the country.
Cairo is the largest city in Africa.

The River Nile runs through Cairo. It is the longest river in the world.

Around 7 million people live in Cairo.

# Land and sea

Most of the land in Egypt is desert. These large areas of sand and rock are very hot and dry. It can be difficult for people, animals and plants to live here.

Thousands of years ago, the ancient Egyptians built huge stone pyramids in the desert.

Egypt has long coastlines in the north and east of the country. Many boats travel to Egypt to buy and sell goods.

Alexandria is the second largest city in Egypt. It is on the north coast.

# 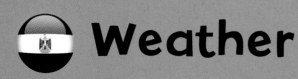 Weather

It is hot and dry almost everywhere in Egypt. There is very little rain. People use water from the River Nile to grow crops.

In some desert areas, it only rains once every five years!

Most towns and cities are built beside the River Nile.

Strong winds blow dust from the Sahara Desert through the air. Every April, a huge dust storm moves across Egypt.

People cover their noses and mouths so they don't breathe or swallow the dust.

# Town and country

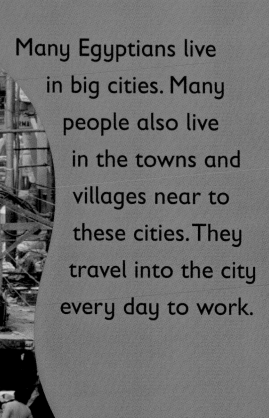

Many Egyptians live in big cities. Many people also live in the towns and villages near to these cities. They travel into the city every day to work.

Luxor has lots of street markets that sell food, clothes and crafts.

Most people in the countryside farm the land. They grow crops such as sugar cane, wheat and sweetcorn. Farmers often do not have much money.

In the countryside, people often use donkeys to carry materials.

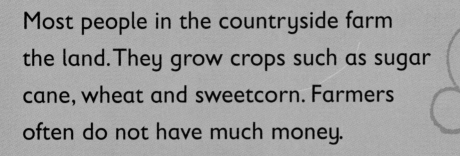

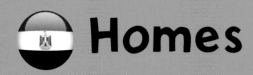

# Homes

Most people in Egypt live in flats.
In big cities, blocks of flats are often
very tall. In towns and villages, people
live in houses or smaller blocks of flats.

Egyptian people have painted their houses
in bright colours for thousands of years.

Bedouin people traditionally live in tents in the desert. These tents are made of goat and camel hair. Many Bedouins today live in houses made of stone or brick.

This Bedouin man is playing a musical instrument called a rebab.

A Bedouin tent is called a bayt.

# Shopping

Egyptian cities have large shopping centres with stores from all over the world. They sell expensive clothes, food, jewellery and many other things.

There are many large new shopping centres in the Nasr City area of Cairo.

Handmade crafts, cloths and perfumes are sold in street markets called bazaars. Sellers talk with customers to decide on a price for their goods.

This man is decorating a gold vase by scratching patterns into its surface.

 # Food

Bread makes up one third of most
people's daily food in Egypt.
The government pays money so that
poor people can buy cheaper bread.

This woman is making traditional Egyptian pitta bread.

Egyptian food uses lots of vegetables and different types of beans. Many dishes are very healthy.

Molokhia is a soup made from green leaves, garlic and chilli.

Dates are sweet fruits that grow on trees in Egypt.

Koshari is a dish of rice, lentils, chickpeas and macaroni with tomato sauce and fried onions.

# Sport and leisure

Camel racing is an ancient, traditional Bedouin sport. It is very popular in parts of Egypt. There is a large camel racing festival in the Al-Sharqiya region.

Camels can run faster than most horses!

Lots of people, especially tourists, go scuba diving in the Red Sea. People have to be careful not to damage the fragile coral reefs.

This scuba diver has found two clownfish!

Some of the coral reefs in the Red Sea are more than 5,000 years old!

19

# Holidays and festivals

Eid el Kabir is a religious festival celebrated by Muslims. It is also called Eid al Adha. Muslims feast, pray and give gifts to the poor.

*Muslims pray together outside in large crowds.*

Shemen Nessim is a spring festival celebrated by people of the Coptic Christian religion. People spend time outside with their families.

Families often enjoy a picnic together in city squares and parks.

# Speak Arabic!

| | |
|---|---|
| **Mar ha-ban** | Hello |
| **Ma-a sa-la-ma** | Goodbye |
| **Min fad-lik** | Please |
| **Shuk-ran** | Thank you |
| **Na-am** | Yes |
| **La-a** | No |
| **Ana is-mee...** | My name is... |

The red, white and black stripes on the flag stand for different times in Egypt's history.

# Make a pharaoh headdress

**You will need:**
- One A4 sheet of white card
- One A4 sheet of white paper
- Coloured crayons • Scissors
- Glue • Black pen
- Stapler

Thousands of years ago, kings called pharaohs ruled over Egypt. They wore headdresses made of gold and jewels.

1. Copy these three shapes onto the white card. Use the crayons to colour them in. Cut them out.

2. Glue the two long shapes onto either side of the back of the other shape.

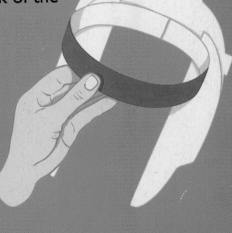

3. Cut out a strip of white paper that is long enough to go around your head. Staple the ends together. Glue this onto the back of your headdress.

4. Your headdress is ready to wear!

Visit our website to download larger, printable templates for this project.
www.waylandbooks.co.uk/popcorn

# Glossary

**ancient** very old

**capital** the city where the government of the country meets

**chickpea** a type of pea-like bean

**Christian** a person who believes in God and the teachings of Jesus Christ

**coral reef** an underwater shelf made of corals, which are sea animals with hard outsides

**crops** plants grown on a farm

**customer** a person who buys goods or services

**Muslim** a person who believes in Allah and the teachings of Muhammad

**pyramid** a three-sided shape with a square base

**sugar cane** a plant from which sugar can be made

**tourist** someone who is on holiday or travelling for fun

**wheat** a plant that has grains which are used to make flour

# Index